THE
ADOPTED FAMILY

Book I

You and Your Child:
A Guide for Adoptive Parents

REVISED EDITION

By Florence Rondell and Ruth Michaels

CROWN PUBLISHERS, INC.   ·   NEW YORK

FIRST EDITION—16 PRINTINGS

REVISED EDITION

Ninth Printing, August, 1972

Library of Congress Catalog Card Number: 51-12008
ISBN: 0-517-50107-4
Printed in the United States of America

CONTENTS

BOOK II: *THE FAMILY THAT GREW*

Acknowledgments

We wish again to express our appreciation to those who helped in the original preparation of this book:

Dr. Viola W. Bernard, who gave generously of her time, interest, and counsel, and contributed the rich knowledge of adoptive families she has gained in her practice as a psychiatrist and in her position as consultant to many agencies in the adoption field, and who gave us advice about various current issues in this area.

Mrs. Berta Bornstein and Dr. Marian Stranahan, who offered invaluable suggestions, comments, and criticisms from their experience as child analysts, and their knowledge of children in both biological and adoptive homes.

Mrs. Ruth Brenner, formerly Director of the Louise Wise Services, who extended her helpful interest and suggestions.

In addition, we wish to thank the following people for their help in the preparation of this revised edition:

Miss Rebecca Smith and Miss Alice Folsom, of Child Welfare League of America, who reviewed the manuscript and offered thoughtful and constructive suggestions.

Dr. David Fanshel, Professor of Social Work (Social Research), Columbia School of Social Work, who shared with us the findings of current follow-up studies of adoption.

FLORENCE RONDELL
RUTH MICHAELS

BOOK I

You and Your Child:
A Guide for Adoptive Parents

Growth of a Family

Every child, whether he comes to his family by birth or adoption, discovers what a family is through the experiences of family living. The newborn infant has no way of knowing which of the many faces that hover about him belongs to a parent. He has no way of knowing what a parent is. He only knows that he is comfortable or uncomfortable, hungry or satisfied.

Gradually, as the months go by, he begins to know who brings comfort when he is uncomfortable, and food when he is hungry. He comes to know the feel of the arm that holds him close when he eats, that holds him safe in his bath. He knows the voice that soothes him and sings to him. He grows to know who will respond to his needs when he calls out. This is the special person in the whole new strange world who belongs specially to him. This is his first understanding of parents—Mother and Father.

The mother and father who care for a child, who listen for his voice and try to interpret what he means, who comfort him, soothe him, feed him and play with him, discover for the first time what it is to be parents. They do not become parents by virtue of conception and birth alone. They grow to be parents, just as the infant grows to know what parents are.

They come to know the developing personality of their child in a way that no other person can really know it. They recognize whether he is a lusty eater or a delicate one; vivacious or reserved;

3

adventurous or cautious. They become the authorities to whom he turns for the answers to everything. They are concerned with meeting his needs and wants, and fostering his growing maturity.

Sometimes, because of their responsibility to their child, all parents have unpleasant things to do. They have to take him for injections. He can have no choice about taking medicine when he is ill. He must learn quickly—and not necessarily "at his own pace"—that gas jets are not playthings. In the intimacies of daily living, the child and the parent learn the bitter and the sweet of family relations.

It is through the experiences of family living that a child and his parents grow to be a family. For every parent, biological or adoptive, it is the daily loving care of the child and his responsiveness that build the parental feeling. For every child, it is being loved and cared for that produces family closeness.

Family by Adoption

The biological and the adopted family alike share pleasant and unpleasant experiences. Parents and child enjoy one another, and at times grow impatient with one another. Day by day, these shared experiences bind them closer, and help the child understand what it is like to be part of a family.

The difference for the adopted family is that their child comes to them by adoption, and not by birth. When the adopted child is the first child in his new family, he comes to a mother and a father who have given much thought and determination to becoming parents. They have already unsuccessfully explored the possibility of having a child biologically. It is their continued deep desire for parenthood that leads them to consider adopting their family.

They have put much effort into the adoption. They have thought and talked about it between themselves, and have discussed the matter with people whose judgment they trust. By the time the child comes to them, he is the fruition of their parental desires and parental efforts. While he is not their child biologically, he is a child who was wanted and planned for, and therefore his family ties develop as do those of any other wanted child.

He becomes part of the larger circle. He is not only the child of his parents, but also the grandchild of their parents. Their relatives become his. He has aunts, uncles, cousins. He is part of family birthdays and celebrations. He has a family which he can turn to, and which can turn to him.

As the child grows, the fact that he came to his family differently from other children assumes its proper perspective, becoming only one part of a rich and full relationship. This happens most easily where the parents help the child to understand the meaning of adoption and its place in the family relationships.

In their daily living, the parents convey their love and enjoyment to the child. Beyond this, they take definite steps to protect him and to make the adoption work. They take necessary legal steps. They interpret the adoption to their own family, friends, and community in a way which safeguards the new parent-child relationship. And they share with their child the knowledge of his adoption, and their happiness with him.

Part II of this book is a story, *The Family That Grew*, which parents can use in many ways to help their child understand his adoption and family relationships. Some of the ways parents may use it helpfully will be discussed in a later chapter.

Preparation for Adoptive Parenthood

In the usual course of events, most people assume that they will eventually have a family. Even children talk of the day when they will be mothers and fathers; and at the time of marriage, couples usually plan to have children.

In thinking of future parenthood, almost everyone can visualize many of the pleasures of family life. Children provide new exciting, common interests and a bond between husband and wife. Parents anticipate the pleasure of watching a child grow to maturity, reflecting their efforts on his behalf, developing as they would like him to. They think of the pride they will take in his personality and in his achievements. They want to be loved and needed, and to see the responsiveness of a child to them.

They feel that in middle age they will relive their youth by watching the development and interests of a child and his young friends. In thinking of the future, too, they look forward to the companionship that a son or daughter will offer. All of these satisfactions of parenthood are so real and so rewarding that people who have had little actual responsibility for children, and who have never taken care of them, often see only the rewards of being parents.

However, those who have given a child daily care and have taken responsibility for him, realize that children not only give parents satisfaction, but also make demands. Under the best of circumstances, there are times when a child will be trying and demanding, a great strain and a great care. There are nights when he cries a great deal, or has nightmares, or doesn't feel well, and his parents' sleep is constantly interrupted. A family may not have a vacation if the child is ill at the time his father is free to go. If a sitter does not arrive, social plans may be upset, even though Father and Mother are celebrating an anniversary or are greatly in need of a night out together. Whether or not Mother has a headache, she has to get up in the morning because the baby needs attention or the older child is ready to start his day.

Although a certain amount of financial responsibility is expected in any family when children arrive, the unexpected financial drains when the family increases to three often cause hardship. Parents may be forced to give up little luxuries formerly taken for granted.

Prior to the coming of a child, husband and wife had only each other to consider. Each was free to give a maximum of attention to the other. With the advent of a child this is no longer so. Father, who always enjoyed fishing trips on his vacation, and Mother, who went along to please him, find that either Father goes alone or the whole family, including the baby, goes along. Mother, who used to enjoy Father's occasional surprises of flowers or candy, finds his surprises now are apt to be dollhouses or spaceships.

Both find that daily living with a child is very different from occasional contact with other people's children. Demands are made on both parents for new adjustments, within themselves and in their relationship with each other.

Couples planning adoptive parenthood have an opportunity to consider what having a child in their home will mean to them, how it will enrich their lives, and what new adjustments it will involve. While they cannot actually experience parenthood in advance, they can see what living with and caring for children might be like for them. They should spend some of their free daytime hours with people who have young children. Occasionally they can have the child of friends or relatives spend a day or a weekend at their home.

For a woman at home during the day there are many opportunities to do volunteer work that will bring her into contact with the actual care of children. Most children's wards, hospital clinics, day nurseries, children's institutions, and settlement-house groups welcome the help of volunteer workers.

Experience with children is useful to all new parents. They can learn what to expect of themselves and of a child, and are therefore freer to enjoy their parenthood.

Once prospective parents have set plans in motion to adopt a baby, they can prepare themselves for parenthood just as any other couple does in the period of waiting for their child. No parent automatically knows the details of caring for a child, what to expect in his development, or how to handle the various emergencies that can arise in daily living. All parents, biological and adoptive, must learn how to do the parent's daily job.

The United States Government's Children's Bureau publishes several excellent pamphlets on the physical and emotional needs of young children, and information about these can be obtained readily by writing to the Children's Bureau, Superintendent of Documents, United States Government Printing Office, Washington, D.C. 20402.

All prospective parents of young babies will want to be familiar with Dr. Benjamin Spock's *Infant and Child Care,* a succinct, readable book about the care of children, by a well-known pediatrician. The courses the Red Cross offers for fathers- and mothers-to-be have proved helpful and practical to many adoptive parents.

Planning for a baby's care, once a family is ready to adopt, involves medical consultation as well as practical knowledge. Any family taking a child for adoption should be sure that a competent physician has examined the baby, so that they know his physical condition and medical needs. Of course, once the baby is in the home, they will have their own doctor supervise his schedule and care.

The mother who has had very limited experience with caring for babies may want a more experienced woman to teach her how to care for her child. Just as biological mothers returning from the hospital after giving birth often want the help of a relative, a friend, or a practical or visiting nurse to start them in their care of the baby, so adoptive mothers may seek such help and support.

For nobody, after all, is a "born parent." Everyone learns to be a parent as a result of his own life experience, the information he has accumulated, the facts he has observed, and the actual living with and caring for a child.

Legal Protections for the Adopted Family

Whenever parents take a baby to be their own, it is important that they protect him by going through the formal procedure which makes him permanently theirs by law. Although the legal adoption does not make them love him more, it does very genuinely protect him and the family life they share together. Legal adoption gives the child the right to the parents' name, and makes him legally their child.

In the very process of adopting the child legally, therefore, the parents assure him of his status as a rightful member of their family, entitled to all the rights that all children have within their family. At the same time, they of course protect their position as his parents. It is formally established that his biological parents surrendered all the rights of parenthood, and that the adoptive parents, and they alone, are his parents, with the rights, responsibilities, and rewards that go with parenthood.

State laws differ in the exact protections they afford adopted children. At the present time, for example, there are still differences in inheritance regulations. The requirements for the completion of an adoption also vary from state to state. Some have minimum age requirements for adoptive parents. Several require that the child be adopted by parents of his own race or religion.

Because there are a variety of considerations, many of them technical, it is always advisable for a family to employ a lawyer to handle the legal aspects of adoption. To avoid delay, expense, and legal complications, investigations must be made and papers drawn according to the technical procedures of the state in which adoption is taking place.

The family lawyer ascertains in advance the special procedures and protections of the state in which the adoption petition is made. He may obtain all necessary information from the Children's Bureau, United States Department of Health, Education, and Welfare, Washington, D.C.; the State Welfare Board in the state where the adoption is to take place; or the social agency that placed the child for adoption. He can explain clearly to the family the steps they will have to follow.

Many adoptive families have had reason to be grateful to the family lawyer, who helped them consummate the adoption effectively and quickly. His expert and thorough legal exploration of the technical requirements saves precious time and avoids redrawing papers or undergoing difficult and tense experiences because of questions arising at the last moment.

A lawyer is able to advise adoptive parents how best to validate the adoption and protect the child within the appropriate state laws. He informs them whether the birth can be registered in their name at the time of legal adoption, or whether some other provision can be made to protect the privacy of the original birth certificate and the information on it. Sometimes there is a choice about the state in which adoption proceedings may be begun, and the lawyer can then help select the one which affords maximum protection to the family and to the child. Where the law does not fully protect the inheritance rights of adopted children, the family lawyer can advise parents how to draw wills that protect these rights completely.

All states have recently tended to increase the protections offered to adopted children. The "probation" period before any legal adoption is consummated is one of these protections. In all states now some time must elapse between the time the child comes to his new family and the time the court allows legal adoption. Many require a court or social agency investigation before an adoption is made final. Such procedures are set up as safeguards for both parent and child, so that the court, in ratifying the adoption, is putting its official permanent seal on a going family and a solid parent-child relationship.

Because new and better legislation may be introduced even long after legal adoption, the family should arrange to keep in touch with the lawyer. He can then advise them how to take advantage of any additional legal protection.

Setting the Social Scene

Even though legal adoption does not take place immediately, the child begins to take root in his family from the day of his arrival. His parents' concern and interest in him begin from the time they take him home to be their child. The way they explain his coming to their family, their friends, and their community is one of the basic protections they afford him.

There is a growing public interest in adoption. Many people who want to adopt children have been unsuccessful. Many more are considering adoption. Most people know adoptive families, and those who are interested in adopting.

The arrival of a new child is always an event, not only to his own parents, their families, and their friends, but also to the community. The arrival of an adopted child stimulates even more interest and curiosity. Whereas with the biological child the mother's pregnancy serves its own notice, usually, outside of a small intimate circle, the community is not aware that an adopted child is expected in a family. Neighbors are therefore apt to be surprised and curious.

Some of the people in the community ask direct questions about the baby; but whether or not they ask, they know a child has been adopted, and they discuss it. Even in a new neighborhood, although they are not in the confidence of the adoptive parents, there may well be people who are aware that this is an adoptive family. Therefore, practically speaking, some announcement from the adoptive parents themselves is appropriate at the time the child arrives.

The adoptive parents are best qualified to allay curiosity and speculation. They can explain that they have been thinking of adoption for some time, and that they were fortunate in obtaining this child. The very fact that they announce their good news makes evident their pleasure in adopting a child. They become a family like any other, and the fact of adoption is accepted by the community. This makes for an easier, less strained living situation for both parents and child.

Introducing the New Family Member

A new addition to the family is always a momentous occasion. Everybody wants to meet a new family member—whether bride, bridegroom, or baby. Engagement and wedding parties afford opportunities to introduce new husbands and wives, but it is impossible for parents to have all their family and friends meet their new baby at once. New parents therefore usually spread their news by sending announcements through the mails, printing a notice in the local newspaper, or often just by telling people themselves.

There may also be religious ceremonies appropriate to the faith of the family.

Adoptive parents can avail themselves of any of these traditional methods. For some people, the simplest way is the use of announcements. If you wish, any form of birth announcement you find appealing and attractive can be adapted for announcing your baby's arrival by the addition of the date on which he came to you. This makes the adoption self-explanatory.

Because so many people are interested and curious about adoption and adopted children, new adoptive parents are frequently besieged with questions, many of them extremely personal. Sometimes people ask where they got their baby, what they know about the biological parents, and under what circumstances the child was surrendered for adoption. These are intimate details the family may rightly prefer not to discuss.

Some Suggestions for Cards or Notes Announcing Adoption

Mr. and Mrs. George Robinson

ANNOUNCE THE ADOPTION
OF THEIR DAUGHTER

Judith Ann

Born: *September* 22, 1966   Arrived: *December* 28, 1966

John and Helen Horner
Welcome the arrival of their son

David Michael
age 2 months
on
October 15, 1966

Edward and Eleanor Brown
are happy to welcome
their daughter Susan

Born: June 6th, 1963
Arrived: August 2, 1965

Adoptive parents are properly concerned about what information they should give people beyond the announcement itself. In the early interest and excitement of having a new baby, it is difficult to foresee what facts should be shared, and with whom. Parents therefore should be highly selective in discussing the child's biological background and the circumstances of his adoption with anyone.

After all, except in the adoption of older children, a few years must elapse before the baby reaches the age when his adoption can be discussed with him in any detail. It is important to remember, however, that it is natural for people to wonder, and to ask specific questions about the background of the new baby. They often do not stop to think that they may be asking for information that is highly personal. Adoptive parents do not have to feel "on the spot," and called upon to provide details. On the contrary, the simpler the information they give others, the less the likelihood that it will become confused.

It is therefore wise for adoptive parents to give no details at all. They have every right to say that they have been assured the background is good and right for them, and they are quite satisfied. They can frankly tell even close relatives that they have been professionally advised, in the best interests of their child, to avoid discussing details with anyone. Most families can accept this. All new parents must begin early to make their own family decisions. Relatives and friends take this for granted or quickly learn it, for they too have had to make decisions in raising their children.

Adoptive parents should, however, convey to everyone their complete and unqualified welcome of their child, and their pleasure in the addition to their family. It is in this way that new parents communicate to others their feeling for the child and their sense of being a family unit. Their family history, like their family album, grows quickly. The essential enjoyment of parenthood is readily understood by others, and is helpful to child and parents alike.

Adoption and Your Community
Through the Years

As the baby grows, the parents' circle of acquaintances grows too. They make new friends, have new neighbors, deal with new storekeepers. Before they know it the child is making his own friends, whose parents, in turn, widen the family's social circle. Adoptive parents sometimes wonder if they should tell each new person that theirs is an adoptive family.

There are occasions when it is appropriate and simpler to mention the adoption. For instance, when mothers talk about their pregnancy or labor, or compare obstetricians or hospitals, it often is simpler and more comfortable for the adoptive mother to make it clear that her child came into the family through adoption.

It is wise to advise a child's doctor of the adoption so that he will not, for example, jump to the conclusion that the youngster's sniffles may be due to hay fever because both adoptive parents suffer from it!

It is neither necessary nor advisable, however, for adoptive parents to make a point of telling everyone they meet about the adoption. Nobody discusses all family business with everyone. Close friends usually share many personal details of their lives with one another, and adoption is a personal detail, like others. Casual acquaintances, on the other hand, do not usually exchange family intimacies, and there is no reason to discuss the adoption

19

with them. If, for example, a waitress in a restaurant where the family is dining comments that the child looks like the father, this may well be true, and does not require an explanation.

Adoptive parents do not need rigid rules about this, any more than about other things. Where they feel it appropriate to mention the adoption, they can do so freely. Where they feel it inappropriate, they can treat it as they would any other personal matter.

Whenever a parent talks about adoption in the child's presence, he should be careful to give only the information that he has already shared with the child. Even a toddler understands more than adults sometimes give him credit for. Just as he understands more words than he is capable of expressing, so the child may grasp more of what adults are saying than they realize, even when he seems to be busy about his own affairs. Many a mother has been unexpectedly embarrassed by a too wide-awake youngster. Although he seems to be happily building a block house while his parents comment critically about a neighbor, he may very well later ask the neighbor, innocently, "Why doesn't Daddy like you?"

This is as true of adoption as of the many other subjects of personal and family interest people talk about at times, forgetful of children present. Peter had been told by his adoptive parents that they had always wanted a little boy just like him. While he was digging a hole to China one day, his mother mentioned to a friend that she had always wanted a girl, but took Peter when he was offered to her, and was very happy she had done so. Weeks later, when she had forgotten the incident, she was taken by surprise when he asked her, "Why did you want a little girl instead of me?" Only then did she realize that her innocent remark had been a cause of worry to her son.

In time the child's social world grows. He not only begins to make his own friends, but now brings them home. He may go to a play group, nursery school, or kindergarten, and later he will enter school. Though parents introduce him to these new experiences, he is moving gradually into a world that his parents cannot completely control, and where they cannot always be with him.

Adoptive parents are often concerned about whether they should inform the responsible adults in each new setting that theirs is an adopted child. Having taken steps to protect him by telling the family, the neighborhood, and the child himself of his adoption, they wonder whether telling the group leader or the teacher will afford additional protection.

Naturally, if the question is specifically asked, they will say that their child is adopted. Parents can discuss between themselves what purpose it would serve to volunteer the information when the question is not asked. In most situations, it is irrelevant, serving no purpose. In the course of his friendships and group and school experiences, it is entirely possible that he himself will mention his adoption. His parents have been helping him to understand that his adoption is simply one fact or experience in his life. If they have done this successfully, he will feel free to mention it where it seems appropriate to him. His friend or teacher may then make some comment to the parents, or ask about it. They will of course acknowledge the adoption, although they need not answer detailed personal questions.

To deny it, whether or not the child is present, would imply to him as well as to the inquirer either that he has lied or that the adoption is a shameful secret. Parents will want to back their child up, and to reinforce his conviction that his adoption was a happy event in his family.

Comfort, appropriateness, and purpose to be served determine the family's selection of those to tell about the adoption throughout the years. They are really the child's criteria too; and the parents should know that he will mention it where it is comfortable for him, seems appropriate to him, or serves his purpose.

Introducing Your Child to Adoption

The adoptive parents begin their protection of the parent-child relationship by taking the proper legal measures, and by interpreting the adoption to friends, relatives, and their social community. Also, from early childhood, they help their child to know and to understand how their family came to be. His growing comprehension that his parents adopted him because they wanted him very much ensures support to the child, and to their family closeness.

All growing children look to their parents as their primary source of knowledge, not only about the world around them, but also about themselves and their own place in it. Parents who discuss adoption with their child are helping to build and solidify his confidence in them.

All parents want a relationship with their child built on mutual trust and confidence, and they try in different ways to develop it. This is why they do not assure him the injection "won't hurt" when they know it will, or make a promise they do not intend to fulfill. This is also why, from his infancy, they do not lie to him just because it seems the easiest thing to do at the time. They are more concerned with protecting the trust and confidence between them than with avoiding a momentary discomfort.

Until the parents have begun to discuss his adoption with their child, they may well be concerned over whether he will get the information in a hurtful way. Although this does not in-

22

evitably happen, sooner or later some member of the family, some neighbor, or some child who assumes he already knows, is very apt to refer to the adoption. This is quite likely since many people assume today that adoption is no secret in a family.

For example, a mother out walking with her little girl in a new neighborhood met an old neighbor she had not seen for years. The neighbor beamed at the youngster and said, "My, what a darling child! Is this the little baby you adopted when you lived near me?" Sometimes a youngster learns of his adoption through children in the family. One little boy was asked by his young cousin, "My Mommy says you were adopted. What does that mean?"

Such incidents can be very disturbing to a child who is completely unprepared. Because the adoption has never been mentioned at home, he may think it is a secret he is not supposed to know about, and he may then be afraid to raise any question about it with his parents. He does not really know, unless his parents have told him, what adoption means in their family life. He therefore has no way of knowing that an adopted child, like any other, is very much the child of his parents, and a permanent beloved part of his family group. He can only assume that his position with his family is somehow precarious—a false assumption that can cause him and his parents much needless unhappiness.

Serious problems may result when the child learns of his adoption for the first time from an unfriendly outsider, who blurts it out in a moment of anger. For example, Joan, a nine-year-old with no inkling of her adoption, had nightmares for weeks after the mother of a playmate she had pushed reprimanded her by saying, "If you don't behave yourself, I'll tell your mother to send you back where you came from!" Her first knowledge that she was adopted implied to her that an adopted child is not a real or permanent part of her family. How could she then dare to ask her parents whether it was true that she was adopted? If they said "Yes," her fears of being turned out might be confirmed because she could not be sure that she was their adopted "real" child for always.

The adoptive parents who have prepared their child have helped him cope with such situations with more confidence. He gains security in learning from his loving parents that he is adopted, and in knowing that his parents are richer and happier for having him. There is no secret between them to block his expression of any concern that he may have about his adoption. There is no network of confusion and suspicion arising from half-heard references, only half understood. Only the child's parents can convey to him the important knowledge that his adoption was a happy event in their family. This is information basic to the emotional climate so necessary for his development.

It is important to remember that the free flow of communication between parents and their children is a precious thing, an important foundation in the building of confidence between them. Therefore, parents who discuss adoption with their child are helping to build and solidify his confidence and security. In withholding this crucial information, they are unwittingly setting up a taboo that endangers the freedom of the two-way communication they rightly value.

These facts are in striking contrast to one of the frequent fears of parents—that in bringing up the subject of adoption, they may imperil the closeness of the parent-child relationship. In this fear, parents are underestimating the strength that close family ties give to children. In the long run, sharing this important aspect of their life together contributes to the development of such closeness, and therefore to family ties.

There is no formula for parents to use in introducing the subject of adoption with their child. After all, this is not a once-and-for-all pronouncement that begins and ends the subject forever. Parents should help their child understand his adoption gradually, according to his comprehension.

As a youngster, he can grasp only the simplest facts, and not their complex implications. His early knowledge forms a foundation on which complete comprehension can ultimately be built, brick by brick, as appropriate to his growing understanding.

This is a process by no means limited to adoption. It is the way a child gradually develops his understanding of everything about himself and his world. To realize this fully, one need only consider how, over the years of growing up, he came to understand sexual relationships, religion, and family values. Prolonged delay in introducing the subject of his adoption runs counter to this process.

Parents often feel some strain when they anticipate talking with their child about adoption. Before they had arrived at their decision to adopt, most parents experienced disappointments in not being able to bear a child. Similarly, in order for this child to become available for adoption, his biological mother had to arrive at the decision that she could not care for him, and wished to place him with parents who could. It often appears to the adoptive parents that in telling their child he is adopted, they are in a sense bringing out the painful aspects for both of them.

This is an understandable feeling, but it does overlook the reality that in taking this child for adoption, his parents have taken steps to effect a happy solution. They have taken him because they believe adoption will afford them the satisfactions of being parents, and will afford the child the fulfillment of having parents. It is vital for parents to recognize that in talking with their child about his adoption they are actually conveying something positive and constructive for all of them—the achievement of a family.

Each parent will have his own words to convey to his child the meaning of adoption. Any of these ways can be helpful if it is geared to the child's ability to understand, and conveys the reality that through adoption, parents and child have found a family both needed.

Parents should feel free, if they wish, to introduce the word "adoption" in their vocabulary of affection even when their baby is too young to understand the specific meaning of the word.

Affection and protectiveness are conveyed by parents to their child even before words have any meaning to him. He responds to the love expressed in their way of speaking to him, their way of holding him, and their ways of caring for and playing with him.

It is through these early associations that he knows deep inside himself that "Mother" and "Father" are very special, loving, and protecting people.

Parents can begin to show how happy they are about having adopted their child even before he understands what the word "adoption" means. There are two ways by which he learns what any word means. One is through his own direct contact with an object—like his bed, his cup, his spoon, his carriage, his toy. But a small child also learns to understand many words that do not relate to objects around him, but to feelings. He knows very early what his parents mean by "good" and "bad." He understands their approval or disapproval even before he knows what he has done to earn it. He knows that "love" and "darling" are warm words that seem to make everyone happy; they make him happy, too. Before he can even pronounce the letter l, many a youngster hugs and cuddles his teddy bear or doll, coming as close as he can manage to "I love you."

The toddler therefore learns about words that describe feelings as well as things. He grasps the feeling behind the word before he really understands what it means. A parent's tone of voice and facial expression tell the child whether the word is pleasant or unpleasant. Even very young children are affected by their parents' attitudes toward many things. The parent who shudders in a thunderstorm, recoils from a dog, and winces at the sight of an insect is unlikely to have a youngster who is relaxed in storms, makes friends with dogs, and enjoys the fuzzy feel of caterpillars. In the same way, his parents' feelings about having adopted him will also color his feelings about it.

Similarly, a young child who hears the word "adopted" used about him in a warm and loving way knows that this word expresses something his family is pleased about. Parents can find occasional opportunities from time to time to include this word in some of their affectionate play with their child. In the child's mind, "adopted" can then become a loving word, connected with being wanted and cherished. His early feelings about himself and his family make a real and lasting impression on him.

It is really for this reason that many parents may wish to

introduce the word early, so that their child's beginning feeling about "adoption" colors his later understanding of it. This is one of the ways that parents can help the child, in this early period, to develop the personal association of adoption with love. Other parents prefer to postpone using the word "adoption" until the child has a basic vocabulary, and some understanding of language.

Parents sometimes feel they are expected to refer to the adoption repeatedly. It is of course important to remember that since adoption is only one aspect of their life together, describing the way their family grew, it would be inappropriate to overstress this.

It has been said earlier that helping a child understand the meaning of his adoption is a process extending through the years of his growing up, and not an isolated episode. Certainly his understanding becomes much more real when he knows that all babies are born, including himself, and that he came to his parents after his birth. Youngsters who do not understand this can feel strange, not because they were adopted, but because they conclude they were never born. As one little girl expressed it, "Johnny was born, but I was adopted."

The ways parents will find to help their child build his understanding will be different, and personal for them. The words they use, at any point, will be those that come naturally to them, words their child understands. Any words which convey that adoption is a happy thing, which has made it possible for them to be a family, will be helpful.

There are some expressions in popular usage which, on the whole, are better avoided. For instance, it was at one time accepted that the idea of a "chosen" baby conveyed the important quality of being a baby "just right" for this family. The intention was a valid one. However, it has been found that for some children this can be a source of confusion—and sometimes even frightening. What if his parents decide they chose wrong? Just as he was "chosen," might he not someday be "un-chosen"?

Also, the concept of a baby "chosen," in this sense, does not really help to convey the two-way street in which adoption has made it possible to meet the needs of parents and child alike.

27

Just as parents find their own words, so will they find their own opportunities for talking about adoption. For example, a relative or a neighbor may adopt a child. Possibly there is another adopted youngster in their own child's nursery, or in their neighborhood. Another opportunity is afforded if they themselves bear or adopt a second child.

Usually, by the time he is five, a child has begun to ask questions about where babies come from. Sometimes he asks about himself, sometimes about the child next door, the neighbor's new baby, or even familiar animals. There are children, however, who for one reason or another do not raise questions of this kind, but nevertheless are curious about how they came into the world. Their parents can create an opportunity to satisfy that curiosity. For instance, they can call attention to the pregnancy of a friend, relative, or neighbor, and explain that a baby is growing inside of her.

Simple explanations are the most appropriate for a young child's first understanding of how his life began. This is the parents' opportunity to help him better understand the world he lives in. Every child needs help from his parents in understanding how everything starts to grow. He has to learn that just as a male and a female horse start every colt growing, and a male and a female cat start every kitten growing, so a male and a female human being start every baby growing. He has to learn, too, that the human baby, like the others, starts growing inside a female.

Wise parents answer their child's questions, realizing that he is trying to learn more about himself and his world. Their attitude increases his confidence and trust so that he feels free to bring further questions to them, and knows that he can rely on their answers. They are further strengthening the parent-child relationship.

In helping their child understand how life begins, adoptive parents are at the same time preparing him to understand the meaning of adoption. Parents can now discuss with him how he came to be part of his family.

Use of the Story Book:
The Family That Grew

Many parents have found it helpful to tell their child in story form the way their family grew. *The Family That Grew*, Part II of this book, provides a framework for such a story.

Circumstances drawn from their own particular family life can easily be substituted for those here, or added to them to make the story more dynamic and alive for their child. For instance, *The Family That Grew* tells of the adoption of a first child. Parents who already have one or more older children will want to adapt the story accordingly.

Similarly, they may want to talk of how old their child was at the time of adoption, how sweet the little boy's smile, how bright the little girl's eyes. It is fun for the child to know what admiring friends and relatives turned out to greet him, and what gifts they brought to welcome him. He is likely to cherish the teddy bear that his Aunt Agnes brought him, or the quilt that Grandma made for his crib. Any youngster relishes stories of his early cute and bright remarks, which can also be included in this context. Whatever personal details parents include, the basic story told here can serve as a guide, for it is designed to help the child with his understanding and acceptance of his own adoption.

In introducing this story to their child, as in initiating any other discussion of adoption, the parents should choose a happy time, when they and he are feeling close and warm. Preferably, they would begin this when both parents are at home and can talk with their child about the story, filling in personal details with him.

The language of this story has been carefully selected because it is the language of a very young child. For example, the biological parents are referred to as "a man and a lady." They are not referred to as "a man and a woman" because a child thinks in terms of "a lady" before he thinks in terms of "a woman." They are not referred to as a father and a mother, because they are not truly able to be a father and a mother. They have never cared for the child as fathers and mothers do. The adoptive parents have cared for him, and are therefore the child's "real" father and mother.

It is good for the adopted child to know he is not unique, and that many other children are also adopted. His parents may comment on the adoption of other children whom he knows. They can tell stories referring to successful adoptions they have known through the years.

The Family That Grew begins by reminding the child that he was born like other children. It assures him that his biological parents would have cared for him if they could; since they could not, they made a good plan for him. This lets the child know again, as his adoptive parents have let him know in many ways, that he is a lovable child, worthy of being cared for, and is a valid addition to their family.

The adoption in this story, like most adoptions, is arranged by an intermediary, a "special person who knows a lot about children and how to make them happy." Knowing this helps the child feel he has been cared for, and placed with the right family. It is also a protection for the adoptive parents and child, when the past history and the present whereabouts of the biological parents are only partially known.

The meaning of adoption becomes clear through the explanation of how the adoptive parents wanted a child very much, and arranged for him to be their child. It describes how he became part of his family, and how his family ties have grown. It tells him, as the adoptive parents themselves have told him in the thousand details of daily living, that they are glad he is

30

their child now. In doing this, the story reinforces the new parent-child relationship, and the value each has for the other.

To understand his adoption fully, a child has to raise questions about it, and have them answered by his parents. It is impossible to know exactly what will puzzle a child in any new experience; whether it is in seeing the ocean for the first time, chasing snowflakes, understanding how he was born, or grasping his adoption. This story affords the child the opportunity to bring out his questions about adoption. Whatever method is used to explain adoption to him, it is important to help him bring out these questions. His ability to do so is healthy, and reflects confidence and trust in his parents, who encourage the closeness between them by answering in terms the child can understand.

Answering the Growing Child's Questions About His Adoption

Sometimes parents feel as if a child is an animated question mark. How else can a child learn about the world he lives in except by asking questions? The adult seeking information can read a book, refer to the encyclopedia, take a course, or consult an expert. The only one of these methods open to the young child is to consult the expert—and the parents are his experts. As he matures he turns increasingly to teachers, to friends, and later to written material to supplement the information received from his parents and his accumulating experiences.

A three-year-old's vocabulary sometimes seems exclusively composed of the word "why." His questions are endless and varied. He is, however, satisfied with simple answers, the only kind he is capable of understanding. When he asks why the car goes, he is content with the answer that the driver makes the car go. If he asks how the driver makes the car go, he can understand that the driver pushes the starter, and that makes the car go. This seems a complete and reasonable answer at this time, but obviously this does not mean that he will not have further questions about cars at a later time.

The ten-year-old, in fact, is frequently interested in learning about the different parts of the car and how they work. He wants further facts and further details. He is now capable of understanding a much more complicated explanation.

When he is in his teens, he may be taking science courses or reading science magazines. Now he can relate his new knowledge and understanding to what he already knows about cars and engines.

All children build their understanding of any subject gradually, as they acquire knowledge and experience. They constantly seek new facts and experiences in order to enrich their picture of the world they live in. The questions they ask and the answers they seek depend on their background of information, and the stage of growth they have already reached.

For example, this is how a child develops his knowledge of sexual relationships. When he first asks where babies come from, his questions are simple and simple answers satisfy him. A child may ask: "Where did Aunt Helen and Uncle Bob get their new baby?" His mother may simply say that baby Betty grew inside of Aunt Helen. As his understanding grows, he returns with new and more complicated questions, and asks for fuller and more detailed answers. Even before he reaches adolescence, he wants a factual and scientific explanation of how life begins. By the time he is in his teens, he is beginning to grasp the relationship between men and women and the nature of a loving marriage. Now he is preparing himself for the role he will play in his own family. Actually, however much information he has, he fully comprehends how a couple mate, how they produce a child, and how they grow to be parents to their child, only when he himself is an adult and a parent.

In the same way, the adopted child is at first satisfied to know how he came to his family. As his understanding grows he asks increasingly complicated questions and wants increasingly fuller explanations about his biological parents and how they came to give him up for adoption. The information that satisfies a five- or six-year-old will not satisfy an eight- or nine-year-old; and similarly, fifteen- or sixteen-year-olds will want even fuller answers. On the other hand, it should be remembered that the older child has had more experience with life and with people. Because of his growing maturity, he is better prepared to understand the answers he seeks.

Essentially, when the growing child asks questions about his adoption, there are special things he is trying to learn. His questions will be phrased in various ways, and may be repeated in more complicated forms as he grows. With fuller understanding of what adopted children need to know, parents are better equipped to answer questions, whenever possible, and thus reinforce the child's assurance about himself, his adoptive family, and the world he lives in.

Some of the child's questions will be about his biological parents. Although he may, in a child's words, ask "who" they were, he probably wants to know what kind of people they were. Every human being needs to feel that he was born of essentially good people who wanted him to be happy. This knowledge contributes to a sense of basic worth and self-confidence. The adopted child also needs this assurance from his adoptive parents.

Whatever the specific answers the parents give about their child's biological parents, they should keep in mind this fundamental need. They should at all times convey their recognition of the biological parents as worthy people, whether they are talking to their child, their family, or their friends.

In giving details about biological parents, the adoptive family can be selective. Every family tree is varied. Every family, closely studied, reveals a variety of personalities, and almost every kind of life history. Every family takes special pride in some members, and not in others. Actually, all parents, biological and adoptive, in telling the family history to their child, select what they think will interest him and contribute to his development.

Where adoptive parents have such information, they can tell the child some of the abilities and interests of the biological parents. If the biological father, for instance, was very athletic, or had technical or professional skills, this might be of interest and help to a child. Similarly, if the biological mother liked to sew or knit, or had musical ability, the adoptive parents might want to tell the child about this. In giving specific information about biological parents, it is well to emphasize those qualities respected and valued in their own family.

Sometimes the child may specifically ask what his biological parents were like. Adoptive parents often find it helpful to stress the resemblances between the biological parents and themselves. For example, where it is applicable, they can point up resemblances in build or coloring. They can also stress general resemblances, even where their knowledge is not detailed. For instance, when a child asks what his biological mother was like, it is possible to answer, "I do not know for sure, but I think she must have been very much like me." This, too, helps to reinforce the child's roots in his adoptive family.

The adoptive family can feel comfortable in accenting these resemblances. The biological parents wanted this child to have the kind of family life they could not provide and the kind of parents they would have wanted to be. After all, no matter what the circumstances under which they surrendered the child for adoption, they did take responsibility for trying to make a plan that would be good for him. In this sense they have provided for him.

Usually, adoptive parents do not know personally the biological parents of their child. Most often an intermediary arranges the adoption and gives the parents their information, so that they do not know every last detail. It is therefore possible that they cannot answer a specific question. If the child asks what has happened to his biological parents—whether they are alive, whether they completed their educations, whether they had other children —the adoptive parents can honestly say they do not know. After all, no parent ever knows everything, and every child has to learn this.

Sometimes a parent may hesitate to share a particular piece of information with his child for fear it might be damaging. In such an instance, he should by all means seek professional consultation on what to do about this.

In raising a child, there are sometimes other situations as well when expert help is best. These usually arise when personal experience, the advice of friends, and generalized information seem inadequate to enable parents to resolve the problem in hand. Professional consultation is provided by social agencies, social workers, psychiatrists, and psychologists.

Every adopted child, sooner or later, wonders how his biological parents came to give him up. When a child asks this, he is seeking reassurance that they really were not able to take care of him for reasons outside their control and his. He needs to feel that they would have cared for him if it had been possible. He may also wonder whether there was something about the kind of baby he was that made them give him up. Everyone wants to feel that he has always been, from birth, an acceptable and lovable human being.

This, then, is a second need that can guide parents in answering their growing child's questions. In discussing why he was available for adoption, they can express their belief that the biological father and the biological mother could not be parents to him for reasons beyond their control, and that these reasons had nothing to do with the child himself.

Most often, adoptive parents do not really know all the circumstances that led to their child's surrender. When they are uncomfortable about this, they are apt to anticipate that he will be uncomfortable, too. At times, they seek to invent an explanation which they hope will be comforting and even conclusive. While at first glance this may seem a ready solution, in practice it raises problems.

A solid parent-child relationship cannot really be built on a foundation of inventions. A child's trust in his parents is learned from their life together, and the sincerity with which they have tried to share with him matters basic to their family life. This, in the long run, is what provides comfort to a child.

Much of the difficulty many adoptive parents have in talking with a child about this stems from the fact that it is difficult for them, who have so wanted a child, to understand how any biological parent could give one up. The adopted child, who has found out how important he is to his parents, also finds this hard to grasp. For something so complicated, there is no simple, conclusive, and completely acceptable answer. It is nevertheless possible, when a child asks questions, to give him some of the reassurance he seeks.

The best answer of all, as many adoptive parents have found, is to say appropriately and honestly, "I don't know exactly why, but I am sure there must have been a very powerful reason." For the child who does not yet understand the word "powerful," "good" or "important" might be substituted, according to his vocabulary and understanding. At the same time, it is advisable and valuable to stress the meaning that adoptive parents and child have for each other, and the importance of their life together as a family.

It is possible that a child will continue to press for a more specific answer, saying, "Give me a 'for instance,'" or "But what could be a good reason?" When this happens, it is natural for adoptive parents to try to find a satisfactory answer. It is important to realize, however, that whatever answer they offer will lead only to further questions, and cannot really satisfy the child fully. For example, if they say the biological mother was too ill to care for him, the child will wonder, whether he expresses his questions in words or not, what was the matter with her; why his father or his grandparents couldn't provide care for him; what was the terrible illness; wasn't it possible that she would get better? One question has to lead to another, because he is really wondering if any reason is so "good" that no way could have been found for them to keep him and care for him. It is only in adulthood that a person can comprehend that even parents, powerful though they seem to a child, cannot always control life as they would want to ideally.

Although the child naturally wonders about his biological parents from time to time, they are not his "real" parents now. It is because they could not be parents to him, for whatever reasons, that they surrendered him for adoption. It is the adoptive parents who have become his "real parents for keeps" by the time the question arises. It is therefore important for them to stress both that they are his "real" parents, and that he is their child permanently, no matter what happens.

They are so much his real parents that the child sometimes wishes he had been born to them. It would, indeed, have been simpler. For the same reason, the adoptive parents, too, sometimes wish that their closeness to their child had included conceiving and bearing him. A child who expresses feeling about this is not wishing he were with his biological parents; he is wishing he had

37

been born to his adoptive parents. The closeness between them stems from their lives together and their love for one another, not the accident of birth.

Parents who recognize this are more at ease and better able to handle their child's questions. This is illustrated by the experience of an adoptive mother whose six-year-old said, "Mommy, I wish I grew inside of you." She answered honestly, "I wish so, too, but that isn't what makes me your Mommy and you my child. I am your Mommy and you are my child because of the way we love each other, the many things we do together, and the way we enjoy each other." When the child answered, "O.K.! Let's have a party!" this mother understood that the matter had been settled to his satisfaction for that day. She also knew that since children learn by repeated experiences, he would in all likelihood return to this question at some future date.

By the time a child raises questions about his adoption, he is usually a deeply entrenched member of his family, the only family he has ever had. It is essential to recognize that the child adopted as a baby has no tie to the biological parents. The adoptive parents are truly his only "real" parents because they are the only ones with whom the child has shared the developing life-experience that helps him grasp what parents are.

They are the only "real" parents for another reason, too. The biological parents have never been mother and father to this child. It was because they could not, for whatever reasons, take on the responsibilities and pleasures of parenthood, that they attempted to find parents for him through adoption. In surrendering the child to the adoptive couple, they acknowledged them as the child's rightful parents from that point on. The process of legal adoption has confirmed society's recognition of this fact.

Occasionally an adopted child asks where his biological parents are now. He may be curious about this, and his question does not necessarily reflect a tie to or longing for "parents" he has never known. Almost always the adoptive parents do not know the whereabouts of the biological parents. They can tell the child that they do not know, and they should tell him, too, that they are his "real" parents because of the maternal and paternal love they feel for him. This assurance from his adoptive family is realistic and helpful for the child.

There are some children who ask very little about their adoption, and seem to be uninterested in it. They may never refer to the subject after early family discussions. Sometimes parents mistakenly think that this is because the child's understanding is complete, and the subject is therefore finished for him. They may be startled, as were Amy's parents, when several years after they thought they had fully explained her adoption, she asked them what "adopted" meant.

Because children learn gradually, little by little, they need to clarify their understanding of their adoption from time to time over the years. Just as parents find opportunities to open the subject of sexual information when their child seems too disinterested for too long, so adoptive parents find natural opportunities to reopen the subject of adoption when their child does not do so himself for a very long period.

It is possible to do this, for instance, by commenting that an acquaintance of the family's is adopting a baby, "just as we adopted you," or by referring to a magazine article about an adopted child, "just like you!" This gives the child an opportunity to review in his own mind and with his parents his status as their beloved child, whom they adopted.

Parents who have a biological and an adopted child sometimes wonder how best to explain their family relationships to both children. They want the biological child to feel he is a beloved member of their family, but they want the adopted child to feel the same way. They feel that both are their "real" children; and they want both children to see them in turn as "real" parents.

When there are biological and adopted children in the same family, they learn about their family relationships from the way that their parents feel about them and act toward them. From what their parents tell them, they learn that they were born in the same way, that they came to their family differently, and that their family relationship is the same as that of all parents and children.

Both learn from their parents how all babies are born, including themselves. Both learn from their parents that they are wanted children.

Since both children will naturally wonder why one came into the family biologically and one by adoption, this is best explained to them factually.

Where the biological child is older, the parents can explain that they adopted a second child because their first one was so satisfying to them. After he was born, his mother and father found out how wonderful it was to have a child in the family. They and the child enjoyed one another so much that they wanted to have a second child as soon as possible. However, another baby would not grow inside the mother. They decided, therefore, that they would adopt a baby so that they could have a larger family.

Where the biological child is younger, both children can be told that the parents could not have children biologically at the time of adoption, and wanted to start their family without waiting longer. They are glad to have two children now because they enjoy being their parents.

Whenever a new baby comes into a family by birth or adoption, an older child needs repeated reassurance of his parents' continuing love. Any child who is accustomed to being the family "baby" and to having his parents' special attention is reluctant to share his privileged position with a new baby. As children in a family grow, their basic affection for each other grows, too. Nevertheless, it is natural for all brothers and sisters to disagree at times, and fight with one another. Sometimes each clamors for the lion's share of the parents' attention. This is entirely normal and exists where there is the best and closest "family feeling."

Certainly all parents want each child to feel sure of his place in their affections. Parents often try to achieve this by treating both children in exactly the same way. They feel that being treated exactly alike will make the children feel they are equally loved. Actually, however, it is neither possible nor appropriate to treat two different children in exactly the same way. A five-year-old requires a different bedtime from an eight-year-old. An eight-year-old requires some recognition that he is growing up, some special privileges, and a larger share of responsibility than a five-year-old. Then, too, the needs and interests of a little girl will probably differ in many respects from those of a little boy.

Although the play of small children is not conspicuously different for boys and girls, as they mature the boy takes increasing pride in his growing strength where the girl takes pride in her developing femininity. The growing girl is likely to want to do what her mother does—she wants to bake a cake like Mother, to shop with Mother, to try on Mother's high-heeled shoes. The growing boy, on the other hand, usually does not want to "hang around the kitchen" unless he can lick the spoons or eat the hot cookies. He very likely loathes trying on new clothes, though he takes pride in his mannish shirt and tie. Where his sister tries Mother's lipsticks and nail polish, he imitates Father's shaving routine. Parents will want to encourage their daughter's femininity and their son's manliness.

"Equal" treatment for two children in the same family therefore means treatment taking into account the age, sex, interests, and personality of each. Although the parents may act differently toward the children, they love both. They are taking parental responsibility in a way both children can recognize. They may at times protest what appears to be unequal treatment, but ultimately they will understand the reasons and their parents' love for both.

This is so whether the family is composed of biological children, adopted children, or a combination. Devoted parental care in daily living best teaches children that they are beloved members of their family.

Adoptive parents, in answering their children's questions about adoption as in all other family matters, individualize according to each child's needs. The specific answers will vary according to the child's age, vocabulary, understanding, maturity, and the form his question takes. However, when parents are aware of what every adopted child needs to know about his adoption, they phrase their answers so as to build and reinforce their family relationship.

Adolescence in the Adopted Family

By the time a child reaches adolescence, he should be well entrenched in his adoptive family and his confidence and security with his parents should be solidly grounded. The well-loved child who understands his adoption still raises questions about it from time to time, but his questions now are part of the attempt all adolescents make to re-evaluate their place within their families and in the world at large. Actually, by this time the adopted child, like all children, is a part of the whole large family of grandparents, aunts, uncles and cousins to which his parents belong, and his ties and roots within it are well established.

Nevertheless, the relationship between him and his parents which has run smoothly until now may seem suddenly less smooth. Parents are apt to find their customary ways of handling their child are not so successful any more. He is likely to be less compliant and to question their authority increasingly. Clashes between them occur with mounting frequency. Sometimes it seems that forceful disagreements arise without provocation and in spite of his parents' exercise of tact and consideration.

Adoptive parents sometimes begin to wonder what is wrong between them and their child. They find it hard to understand him sometimes, because he seems unreasonable, inconsistent, and impossible to satisfy. Occasionally his behavior and attitude seem so different from what they were when he was younger that they hardly recognize their child. Often the parents wonder if the difficulties between them arise because theirs is an adopted family.

It should comfort them to know that biological parents have similar experiences, and sometimes feel their child is alien to them. They also find their youngster is less docile and consistent than he used to be, and that frequently he does not seem to know what he wants from one moment to the next. At time he monopolizes the conversation; at other times he cannot reply civilly to a direct question. He may tackle a man-sized job with enthusiasm, apparently ready to rewire the electrical circuits in the house; or pick up a book and read in semidarkness, refusing to change a bulb. Sometimes he treats his parents' every word as gospel, and at other times he seems to think they know nothing of how the world has changed "since they were young."

Many of the difficulties which adoptive parents experience with their children at this time stem from the nature of adolescence itself, and not from adoption. The adolescent is in a period of transition from childhood to maturity, and is trying to find his place and footing in the grown-up world. Because his behavior is so closely related to the physical and psychological changes he is living through in growing up, it is important to consider those changes as they relate to biological and adopted families alike.

Even before a youngster enters the teens, rapid glandular changes begin in preparation for physical maturity, and these result in dramatic physical and emotional changes. The child shoots up rapidly in size and may well tower over his parents, and this in itself gives him a new sense of strength and power. This vigor stimulates him to tackle new problems energetically, and to seek new and varied experiences. He wants to grow up so fast that he sometimes overwhelms both himself and the adults around him.

The boy's voice begins to deepen, his beard sprouts, and his schedule soon includes frequent shaving. The girl begins to menstruate and becomes conscious of her figure. They are obviously developing into a man and a woman. Naturally, they have a heightened awareness of their own bodies and those of the opposite sex.

At the same time, the adolescent, all through his high-school years, is developing a new and more acute intellectual ability. He begins to put together all the information he has learned in school and to get an increasing sense of the larger world we live in. Through his reading, he comes into contact with new and provocative ideas, experiences, and relationships he himself has never had. As a result, he gets a new grasp of how men and women feel and think.

With this new strength and physical maturity, this new knowledge and understanding, the adolescent feels, often, quite grown up. He feels fully capable of making decisions without interference or guidance from his parents. He is eager to make his own vacation plans, and choose his own school and work plans. Actually, of course, the adolescent needs parental support as much as ever, although often he does not welcome it. If sixteen-year-olds plan an unsupervised trip to another part of the country, their parents will certainly veto such a project as inappropriate and unsafe.

As parents come to recognize that their child is growing up in many ways, and is more capable and independent than he used to be, they should allow him increasing freedom and privacy. Since he considers the letters he writes and receives both personal and private, it is to be hoped that his feeling about this would be respected. It is as important for parents to honor the privacy of his diary and personal papers as for him to respect theirs.

It is important, too, for the adolescent's parents to realize that he needs an opportunity to experiment increasingly with making his own choices and decisions, even though he will necessarily make mistakes. A person who has never made independent decisions in small things cannot develop confidence in his ability to make important decisions. After all, confidence and maturity of judgment are built slowly, through trial and error. Accordingly, parents contribute to the adolescent's development as they offer him opportunities for increasing independence of judgment and decision, wherever this is appropriate.

It is often difficult for parents to understand the decisions and choices made by their adolescent children. In many families, it is hard to figure out, at times, how the youngsters select their friends. A socially inexperienced youngster may select the most sophisticated girl in her class as her best friend. A serious-minded boy may cultivate the friendship of his most nonconformist classmate. The adolescent has the need to experiment with a variety of relationships, and to test out his emerging values and standards. When he is left to experiment freely in choosing his own friends he ultimately discovers for himself the people with whom he has most in common, and who will be his long-time friends. It is only if he becomes involved with someone whose behavior is delinquent or otherwise destructive that the parents have a responsibility to intervene.

Although the sixteen- or seventeen-year-old has reached a stage in his growth where he is ready for more freedom than he ever had before, he continues to need his parents' protection a times. He is growing up, but he is by no means fully grown. It is therefore still appropriate for parents to continue those restrictions which they consider necessary. When a youngster wants to make a major decision which will affect his future, this is the time when he needs parental counsel, sure though he may be that he knows what he is doing. When he wants to leave school, or to change his vocational training or goals, family discussion is necessary to be sure that he is not acting impulsively, and that the change of plans is sound in terms of his own future.

Parents also may find it necessary to exercise some restrictions on an adolescent's plans for work. It can be constructive as well as practical for a high-school teen-ager to work after school, on Saturdays, or during vacations. Parents, however, have a voice as to the suitability of the particular job chosen. If their daughter is inclined to be fragile, they may feel that a job as a waitress, carrying heavy trays, is too strenuous for her.

In ways other than work the adolescent does not yet know the limits of his new physical strength. He would be quite willing to stay up all night and every night working on his pet hobbies and projects, or going out with his friends. Although his experience is much wider than it has ever been, it is still limited enough to require help toward self-control and balanced judgment. Because he is fighting so hard to be grown-up, and because he is unaware of the gaps in his experience, the adolescent is likely to resent bitterly any criticism from his parents, and to rebel against their authority and what he considers their "interference," whether or not he is an adopted child.

However, parents should remember that when their child was learning to walk they offered him protection, even though he was not aware that he needed it, or perhaps even resented it. They did not leave him free to walk down high staircases, or into the gutter, nor did they let him run free in a crowded street or store. It is just as true that the adolescent needs the protection of his parents now, even though he may protest vigorously.

To allow the adolescent increasing freedom of thought and action and yet to afford him a parent's protection is a difficult and delicate balance for all parents, adoptive or biological. They, too, have to adjust to the many changes in their adolescent child's development, and in his social behavior and social world.

All parents in this period are likely to find themselves excluded in many ways from their child's confidences. Where formerly he turned to them for everything, he is now more likely to turn to the judgment of his friends; and the telephone may be tied up for hours in serious consultations. He is not so ready to share everything with his parents and usually insists on his right to privacy. He takes nothing for granted; he prefers learning from firsthand experience.

This is a period when young people have a rapidly expanding independent social life. They go off to the beach, to dance, or to the movies with groups of friends. Many an adolescent girl without a date on a Saturday night has been outraged by her parents' well-meant suggestion that she go along with them. This seems blatant exposure—an announcement of her social failure to any friends she might chance to meet.

Adoptive parents are sometimes concerned about their adolescent child's preference for his contemporaries and for his own social world. They wonder if this is a reflection on the closeness of their family ties.

Every adolescent, adopted or otherwise, however close the family ties, has to establish a new world of his own outside the family as part of his growing up. He wants to test his growing strength, ability, and judgment in a circle in which he is as experienced and capable as anyone else, where *his* judgment is as much to be respected as any other. This is why all parents find their adolescent children relying on themselves and their friends in social matters and struggling to loosen "family apron strings."

Since adolescents value their prestige in their own group so highly, it is important to them not to stand out as conspicuously different from the others. They have a great need to dress according to the current style in their circle, and to sport the current "in" haircut—even though it may, to their bewildered parents, look more "far out" than "in." It is difficult for one youngster to have to return directly home after a school dance when the others go for a Coke or a snack. Remembering their own youth, wise parents take the customs of the group into account in setting the rules for their own youngster.

Parents are always startled the first time a boy calls when their daughter is not home and refuses to leave his name with them. It is hard to realize that their sons and daughters are old enough to pair off. At this age, boys and girls find each other attractive and want to be sought after. They spend endless time before the mirror, experimenting with haircombs and makeup. This is the time, too, when it is normal for youngsters to become interested in the opposite sex, and sexually curious—and what parent does not remember his own similar experience? Boys and girls are getting a foretaste of what manhood and womanhood hold in store for them, and in this sense are preparing themselves for adulthood.

These new social relationships are troubling to all parents. It is natural for both adoptive and biological parents to wonder whether their children are grown up enough to handle themselves responsibly. Every parent wants his child to be guided by values in a way that will enable him to enjoy a sound family life when he is ready. All parents can be sure that when the loving relationship between them and their child has been well established, they have given him sound roots in family life. A well-loved child, secure in his place in his family, has an essential respect for the basic values of his parents, biological or adoptive.

This is hard for parents themselves to realize, because an

adolescent often seems so lacking in respect, protesting their actions and authority loudly and forcefully. However thoughtful and tactful parents may be with their adolescent child, it is to be expected that he will at times protest, and feel that they are interfering. He may accuse them of still treating him like a little child—and sometimes perhaps he is right!

The protests of the adolescent frequently take the form of defiance of his parents, and often result in clashes between them. As mild a thing as a parent's suggestion that he wear a pair of rubbers when it is drizzling and a downpour looks imminent may provoke an outburst of indignation. He feels that such a suggestion is an affront to his dignity, and he is likely to reply that he knows perfectly well how to dress himself.

Whereas he formerly may have objected when bedtime came, he now resents the very idea that anyone would set his bedtime. He has a stock answer for any such humiliation: "You don't understand! You're another generation. Times have changed since you were young!" Even though this is more likely to be part of his personal Declaration of Independence than a relevant statement of fact, parents are indeed faced with the reality that in our rapidly changing world, many changes have taken place in attitudes and mores since they themselves were teen-agers.

In order to prove to them (and sometimes to himself) how capable of independent thinking he is, and how far he has come from the position of a small obedient child, the adolescent may frequently oppose even their most cherished beliefs. He can build elaborate arguments to prove that their religious, social, or political opinions are outdated, and that the opposite beliefs—no matter what they are—are the only modern and intelligent ones. Even though parents realize this is usually a passing phase in their child's growth into adulthood, their exasperation, also natural, can make them forget this sometimes. To all parents there comes the time when their youngster "does not talk like any child of ours." When he is theirs through adoption, they sometimes wonder if this accounts for his difference from them. Actually, most adolescents at times, whether or not they are adopted, express the same sharp opposition to the standards and beliefs of their parents.

It is the force and vigor with which the adolescent expresses resentment and defiance that sound so new and strange to parents. If they think back, however, they will see that this is just a new expression of every child's characteristic way of testing his new awareness and independence. All healthy children assert themselves from time to time with as much force and vigor as they can command at a particular age.

Even in babyhood many children begin to assert themselves by shutting their mouths tight against the food being offered them. The two-and-a-half-year-old has a new and powerful weapon: he knows how to say "NO," and he is likely to say it to many of the familiar routines, sometimes just for the pleasure of expressing his own opinion.

The six- or seven-year-old is no longer willing to go to bed unprotestingly, "like a baby." He prefers to join the adult activities and share in the household's "night life." When he finally succumbs to parental pressures, he gets around them by asking for "another drink of water," "a piece of bread and butter," "just one more story," or company "because he is lonesome."

The nine- or ten-year-old plays hard with his friends and is apt to feel it is "not fair" that he should be called in for meals at the family's convenience.

By the time he is along in his teens, the youngster has his own fixed standard of "what the well-dressed teen-ager will wear," not always appropriate by adult standards for the occasion or even suited to the thermometer. He defends his choices with a defiance born of his new strength and vigor.

At any age level, the child's protest can be forceful. The small child says, "You're a *bad* Mommy and Daddy," or "I don't like you." The older one finds other ways to show his anger. It is always important to remember that such feelings, however forcefully expressed, do no necessarily imply a bad parent-child relationship. They usually represent a small and passing part of the child's feeling for his parents.

After all, no human relationship can ever be completely smooth and loving at all times. Brothers and sisters, however close, have their sharp differences upon occasion. Even husbands and wives, however loving, can at times be annoyed with each other. It would not be human for a parent never to be exasperated or impatient with a child, nor would it be human for a child never to be exasperated or impatient with a parent.

Sometimes the impatience is appropriate and sometimes it is not appropriate at all; both are normal. With only one bathroom in the house, Father and Mother are justifiably annoyed when their daughter takes two hours to make up when all have to get ready for the day's work. When Mother is taking her youngster to a children's party, the child is justifiably upset when the telephone rings, and Mother gets involved in a lengthy conversation.

On the other hand, when Father has had a difficult day at the office, he does not feel sunny and playful; he is often easily annoyed by small things—and, for that matter, by small children. The young girl who has been snubbed by her best boyfriend is likely to be touchy and explosive at the dinner table. Under such circumstances the child may not know why the parent is angry any more than the parent knows what is really upsetting his child.

Just as the parent is no less the loving parent because he is angry, so the child is no less the loving child when he is upset. His defiance of his parents, at any age, is not in itself a reflection on his love. The adolescent who feels very sure of his place in the family can express his anger without fearing that he may lose his parents' love. He needs his parents' continuing affection and understanding, particularly at such difficult moments.

The ability of parents and child to lose their tempers with one another sometimes, yet nevertheless to love one another, is healthy. It makes for stronger family ties because it allows for mutual tolerance and love despite differences of feeling and thinking. It helps a child know what to expect from other relationships —with teachers, employers, friends, even from a future husband or wife. In all his adult relationships he will have to be prepared for the fact that nobody is warm and giving and understanding all of the time. He needs to understand that people can work together well and live together affectionately despite differences of opinion and expressions of temporary anger or annoyance.

The anger that flares up between all adolescents and their

parents, adoptive or biological, is usually temporary. However vehemently an adolescent complains that his parents "don't understand him" and "treat him like a child," he is by no means to be taken literally. He is so eager to achieve adult status that he is impatient with the time it takes to grow up. Nevertheless, he is often partially aware that he is not ready to be entirely responsible for himself and his life. He is not ready, for that matter, to be responsible for leaving the bathroom as he found it, or for keeping the dresser drawers in order. Much as he resents his continuing need for help from his parents, and sees it as a blow to his pride and confidence, he still needs and welcomes the protections they offer. Secretly, he relies on them to prevent him from going too far in the adventuring and experimenting which are normal during this period.

The adolescent has half left childhood behind him, and is half a child still. He has half achieved adulthood and is half aware of how unready he is to take on an adult's responsibilities in the world. It is because he has one foot in childhood and one in the adult world that his balance is precarious. His uncertain state is a problem for him and no less a problem for the parents who live with him.

The adopted child may express the defiance and resentment characteristic of this age by attributing the difficulties between him and his parents to the adoption. However, in every family, adolescents express similar defiance and resentment in some form that they think "hits parents where it hurts." Naturally, adoptive parents should now, as always, take every opportunity to stress that theirs is a "real" parent-child relationship. They should never risk undermining their family ties by attributing any difficulties between them to the fact that the child was adopted.

Every child's adolescence puts demands on the flexibility, imagination, and sense of humor of his parents, but all parents can take pleasure and comfort in their child's growing maturity. His approaching "coming of age" provides a source of pride for both parents and child.

Answering the Adolescent's Questions About His Adoption

By the time the adopted child reaches adolescence, the years of parental affection have nourished his growth as a person in his own right and as a child of his parents. Nevertheless he is, like every other adolescent, re-examining his family relationships, and in the course of doing this he may bring new questions about his adoption. By now he knows that he was born as all children are and came to his adoptive family by the planning of both his biological and adoptive parents. He knows that he is his adoptive parents' wanted and loved child. His questions about adoption now reflect his attempt to clarify his understanding in the light of his growing knowledge, experience, and maturity.

The precise questions that the adolescent youngster may raise are extremely varied. The adoptive parent can be sure, however, that no matter how the questions are phrased, they still are variations of the basic questions with which he is already familiar.

The adolescent asks about his biological parents because he wants to clarify further his own acceptability as a child born to such people. He may raise new questions about how they came to give him up, in his attempt to understand how this could result from reasons outside both their control and his.

The parents are therefore guided by their understanding of the child's basic needs in answering any question that arises, just as described in the chapter *Answering the Growing Child's*

Questions About His Adoption. In all discussion about adoption, now as always, the adoptive parents stress their acceptance of the biological parents as good people with good reasons for surrendering the child.

The adolescent draws on his new knowledge of life and people for a better understanding of how and why biological parents can surrender a child for his own protection. He may, in this connection, ask whether his biological parents were married, because he has learned through his reading that most adopted children are born out of wedlock.

This is a question that is often very hard for adoptive parents to discuss, when they know that this is so.

While they may want to answer factually, they are apt to be concerned about whether such knowledge will perhaps undermine the values and standards they believe in and hope their child will live up to.

As mature people, they know there are many reasons why a child may be born out of wedlock, many circumstances that may prevent a couple from marrying, even when they love each other. They know that sometimes this can happen when young people have not had the stabilizing help and guidance of loving, interested parents.

Whatever the reasons that led to this child's being born out of wedlock, it is usually their hope that he will ultimately have *his* children within the protections of a marriage and a family. After all, it was very probably the hope of his biological mother as well. One of the frequent reasons unmarried mothers decide to give up their babies for adoption is precisely to provide a normal family life for them, so that they can in due time lead normal and happy family lives of their own.

Through the years, the adoptive parents have tried to provide the kind of emotional climate that encourages their child's feeling for family life.

At this point, he needs to know from them that the circumstances of his birth do not reflect on the basic worth of either his biological parents or himself. Since every human being needs to take pride in his own status, they can use this opportunity to

53

help him understand that the fact that biological parents were unmarried in no way affects the character and personality of any child.

The problems of being a child born out of wedlock are really social problems. The laws and customs of our society have been set up to give children a sound and stable upbringing through marriage and the two-parent family. The family that consists of an unmarried mother and her child is sometimes disapproved of, and may stand out as different from the other families in the community. It is a constant reminder that this girl has failed to conform with the approved customs of our society.

Even though the unmarried mother may bring her child up in a completely responsible fashion, most people do not consider this. Instead, they take it for granted that she is generally irresponsible, and unable to train a child according to the soundest traditions of the community. Actually, no child is born with a sense of private property or a respect for the truth. Every child learns standards of right and wrong from his parents as he grows. People are apt to be overcritical of the child raised by an unmarried mother, without the guidance of a father. They tend to overemphasize and misinterpret behavior that is normal for all children.

It is always a problem for a child to be subjected to excessive criticism and unjustified disapproval. The possibility that such problems might arise are diminished when a child is adopted by a married couple. The adoption makes him socially and legally their child, with all of the "rights and privileges" that go with being their child. The knowledge that he is a beloved member of a socially acceptable family is reassuring to any child.

Sometimes an adolescent child may ask where his biological parents are now. Adoptive parents can become needlessly concerned about the possible significance of such a question at this point. It is important to realize that in the course of growing up there are moments when every child feels that his parents do not understand him. When Mother tells Betty she cannot leave for her date until the dishes are done, or when Father refuses Bill extra money when he has used up his allowance, the youngster is likely to feel misunderstood and mistreated. Almost every child, at such a time, feels that his parents are unfair and mean to him, and that surely somewhere in the world there must be the ideal parents who would never cross him.

When the child is biologically theirs, parents can easily see that this is a very unreal, passing, momentary thought. Despite their concern for the child, it may even strike them as absurd enough to be funny. Adoptive parents, however, are sometimes vulnerable about this. They can mistake it for reality, and think that their child is yearning for his biological parents.

A child adopted very young has no real picture of his biological parents, and no idea of what they were like. He has never experienced with them the loving, nurturing care which builds the tie between child and parent. He therefore has no real kinship with them.

Any parents of any adolescent who wishes for the all-sympathetic parents of his dreams are most helpful when they handle this realistically and sympathetically. They can always say that, imperfect as they are, they are the only parents he has; and that they are trying, according to their best judgment, to help their child whom they love. Adoptive parents, like any others, are most helpful to their child in this same way.

In answering the questions that an adolescent child raises about his adoption, the parents are building on the groundwork they have laid during earlier years. They have already helped the child to understand that he is in their family by plan. He knows that his home has been selected especially for him. He has been told that his biological parents planned in this way for his care; and it can be assumed that they considered these the kind of home and the kind of parents they wanted him to have.

Thus the child has grown up knowing that his real roots are in the adoptive family and that they are his "real" parents. Actually, this is the other side of a family picture very familiar to the adoptive parents, who surely know deeply by now that he is their "real" child.

The Adopted Family as a "Real" Family

The adopted family provides parents and child with all of the fulfillment and satisfactions that go with family living, and is therefore in every sense a "real" family. Adoptive parents share with all parents the experience of loving their child and enjoying his love in return. The affection that flows between them creates an atmosphere in which the child's emerging personality can flourish. He can turn to his parents for the protection and encouragement that all children need in their family living. The adopted child finds in his home and family life the climate in which he can grow and develop, just as all other children do.

His parents pass on to him the family anecdotes, family customs, and special family celebrations they themselves learned from their own parents and grandparents. He in turn will pass on this family heritage to the generations that succeed him. The family heritage is a social heritage, and it is learned by living within the family and being part of it.

Adoptive parents offer their child essential emotional richness—the finest gift that any parents can offer. All fathers and mothers want to be the best possible parents. They sometimes feel that to be good parents they must always make the "right" decision, say the "right" thing, and have the "right" attitude about everything; that whenever they do not do that, they have failed the child and themselves. This is an impossible standard for any human being and an unnecessary one from the child's point of

56

view. Where parents really want to help their child, and the feeling between them is basically loving, "mistakes" are not only natural but also insignificant. It is even healthy that parents make mistakes sometimes, because no child could live with infallible parents even if they existed.

All parents at times question their handling of various situations with their children. Sometimes experience itself shows that some other way of handling a particular situation might have been better. Often parents continue to take a child to and from school for a while after he thinks he is able to go by himself or with his friends, feeling that he is not old enough to cross the streets unescorted. It is not unusual for them to find that he is more careful and responsible than they realized, and that other children tease him as a "baby" because he is escorted to school and they are not.

Sometimes, too, parents change their handling of a problem as they themselves read and learn more about better methods of child rearing. Often they continue to feed their child after he can and wants to feed himself, because he makes such a mess of the high chair, his clothes, himself, and the kitchen floor. When they learn that this is the child's way of finding out about different foods and utensils, they allow him to feed himself, and suffer the mess that follows.

No parent ever handles every situation perfectly, and in the light of increasing experience and knowledge every parent learns to do a better job.

It is possible, too, for the best of adoptive parents to feel that they should have answered some questions differently in discussing adoption with their child. This book is not intended to provide an inflexible list of "right" answers, but to help parents understand the child's needs and the meaning of his questions, so that they can discuss adoption helpfully with him in their own way.

For loving parents trying to help their child there are many "right" ways to explain adoption, and every parent finds his own words. Even if he says the "wrong" thing on occasion, the "mistake" will not necessarily damage the child or upset the loving relationship between them. Perhaps, at a moment of uncertainty, parents have given a child misinformation about his adoption. At a later date, they may want to correct this.

In talking it over with him, they can explain that this information was given at a time when they felt he could not grasp the true facts. They can acknowledge that perhaps this was an error of judgment on their part, but that they told him what they thought would be clearest and most helpful to him at that time. Now they feel he is able to understand the actual situation more fully.

This is something that a child can accept without permanent damage. A well-loved child, secure in his parents' affections, is not easily damaged, and a solid parent-child tie is not easily broken. The fabric of family living is strong and permanent, woven of many threads.

Parents can therefore be comfortable in the knowledge that their deep feeling for their child, their concern for his needs in growing, and the family life they share, will more than balance any errors they make. Adoptive parents, like all parents, are human enough to make mistakes, to be impatient and less than perfect, but also, like all parents, they provide their child with the life experience and the love which make him a secure and happy human being, capable of rich family living.